Praise
A Leader's Manual

Lenny La Guardia

Forerunner Books
Kansas City, Missouri

Praise: A Leader's Manual
By Lenny La Guardia
Children's Equipping Center
International House of Prayer

Published by Forerunner Books
International House of Prayer
3535 East Red Bridge Road
Kansas City, Missouri 64137
(816) 763-0200 Ext. 675
forerunnerbooks@ihop.org
www.IHOP.org

ISBN: 0-9776738-6-3

Unless otherwise noted, all Scripture quotations are from the New King James Version of the Bible. Copyright © 1979, 1980, 1982 by Thomas Nelson, Inc., publishers.

Cover design by Tom Morse-Brown
Interior design by Dale Jimmo

Printed in the United States of America

Table of Contents

Welcome

Greetings!

Thank you for making *Praise* and the Glad Heart Resource Series a part of your life and the lives of those you teach and reach for God. At the International House of Prayer (IHOP) Missions Base and the Children's Equipping Center, we hold as one of our highest values that young people today be equipped and grounded in the Word of God and released in praise, prayer, power and the prophetic. As a part of the Glad Heart Resource Series, *Praise* endeavors to assist you as you encourage a generation of young people learn to praise God with all of their hearts, no matter what the circumstances of their lives may be.

We have ministered to children and youth for twenty-five years. We see today, more than any other time, the massive need for a paradigm shift in how we as parents and leaders choose resources and prepare and present teaching lessons to our children and to those we lead. Long ago one of our mentors taught us that the definition of curriculum was derived from the Latin term meaning "course of ground." To understand curriculum, we must understand the course of ground God would have us cover with this generation of children.

Over the many years of serving families and their children, we have always believed that the greatest curriculums and workbooks ever written come directly from the Word of God. In developing the Glad Heart Resource Series, we have adhered to that belief and we have set out to assist young people and their parents and leaders in obtaining godly understanding and theological truth that unlock the human heart to the reality and revelation of the "glad heart of God." That's right – God has a glad heart! We believe God desires to give us fresh vision in raising up and equipping a generation of young people to walk in His truths.

May the Lord continue to give you grace as a communicator of the Gospel as you pursue one of the greatest privileges we can have while walking with Jesus – teaching young people.

Blessings in the Name of the Lord,

Lenny and Tracy La Guardia

Introduction

Bringing the Music and the Message Together

The Glad Heart Resource Series introduces and explores four primary themes through forty lessons and forty songs. Each theme has ten lessons, each accompanied by a song. The four themes are as follows:

- **Praise:** Ten lessons and ten songs to teach young people to give God praise no matter what circumstances surround them. King David described the three responses of people who fear God and put their trust in Him alone: They tremble, rejoice and embrace the heart of God (Psalm 2:2-12).

- **Prayer:** Ten lessons and ten songs to teach young people the reality of God's unconditional love for them and His desire to have a day-to-day personal and on-going relationship with them and all who serve Him. Isaiah 56:7 says, "Even them [the Gentiles] I will bring to my holy mountain, and make them joyful in My house of prayer for all nations."

- **Power:** Ten lessons and ten songs to provide young people with an understanding of God's truths and His desire that they walk in the power of the Holy Spirit, revealing salvation to the lost, preaching and teaching the Gospel, healing the sick and broken hearted, and ministering to the poor. Isaiah 8:18 says, "Here am I and the children whom the Lord has given me! We are for signs and wonders."

- **Prophetic:** Ten lessons and ten songs to teach young people how to develop godly characters and understand how and why God desires to speak to them and through them. Acts 2:17 tells us that in the last days, God's Spirit will be poured out on all flesh and His sons and daughters will prophesy.

Understanding the Glad Heart Resource Series

Each lesson includes a song that corresponds with the lesson. The song and the lesson together make one complete lesson. You, the teacher, will be involved in the following five steps that will assist you in teaching the lessons with passion and clarity.

1. **Reflect** on the theme of "Praise" by completing the personal reflection section prior to preparing each of the ten lessons that support the theme. This section will assist you in getting in touch with your own heart and the hearts of the students.

2. **Listen** to the song that goes with each lesson several times and journal your thoughts and reflections in the template provided. This allows you to make notes about various aspects of the song that can be used in the teaching. Once you feel and understand the meaning of each song, you will be able to teach with greater passion and clarity.

3. **Review** the information about each song and the background of why that song was chosen to be part of the lesson. This will help you become acquainted with the heart of the song. Remember, we don't want our young people just going through the motions when they sing the songs; we want them to take the songs they sing seriously and give praise to God.

4. **Study** and meditate on the biblical content presented in each lesson and examine the lesson objective. This allows you to gain the biblical understanding and revelation needed to communicate soundly the Word of God.

5. **Complete** the lesson preparation template and prepare to present the biblical content and lesson objective. This gives you an action plan.

Personal Reflection on the Theme of "Praise"

This section will assist you in being open and honest and, most of all, approachable to your students. Write your responses to the statements below. Young people desire us to be vulnerable and transparent and we need to open up our hearts and lives to this generation. Many of our most important times of communicating to the young people come when we share personal experiences and areas that are a little tender to us.

Please review the statements and answer the personal reflection questions. Put your heart into this and allow yourself to focus on bringing out your thoughts. What has been tugging on your heart regarding what young people see and face today, what they experience, etc.?

- Today, more than ever, children and pre-teens are bombarded with media presentations, current events, and life situations that communicate a violent approach to justice, love, honor and respect.

  How have you seen things change around you?

- For many young people today it seems as if they are forced to grow up too quickly. Every child deserves to be a child. By our lives and love for God, we can help them keep their eyes on Jesus.

  Do you agree or disagree with this and why?

- Sometimes it is almost too much for some people to bear their life circumstances, so they turn on God and blame Him for what has happened or is happening.

  Have you ever blamed or been angry with God? If so, when and why?

Praise

- For some people, when they turn away from God, they never understand why the walls in their hearts grow bigger and thicker.

  In what areas of your life have you allowed walls to go up?

- It is our hope that as you deliver and bring the message of the Gospel, you do so with love and kindness.

  In the past, when have your words been harsh or when have you been impatient with the young people you were teaching?

- Many young people have deep personal heart wounds from role models who have not modeled the love of Jesus with tenderness and integrity.

  What is your idea of a good role model?

- As a communicator, it is important that you embrace God and give Him praise no matter what your circumstances may be.

  Write about an instance when you gave God praise during a time of crisis, conflict or concern.

- God does not stop loving us based on our circumstances.

  What was the most hurtful time in your life? Is that area still tender? If not, how did you get through it?

- God's love for us goes deep and nothing will stop Him from loving us.

  How would you rate and describe your understanding of God's love?

- *Praise* will help young people praise God for who He is, not based on their circumstances. We want young people to set their sights on the Lord even though the world around them is full of pain and turmoil. For years, much of the Church indirectly taught children to put on fake smiles, sing songs, raise their hands and then go home. Many learned the songs, but never learned to live out the truths the songs conveyed. *Praise* is designed to explore the heart of God and release young people to grow in intimacy with God.

  Write in your journal about how God has changed you and how you have come to the place of giving Him praise no matter what circumstances surround you. Then do the following exercise.

- Make a list of every person to whom you will teach this material.

- Next to each name, write what you know about that person.

- Write how you believe each person sees you as a person and as a communicator of the Word.

- Write down what changes you plan to make in relating to and communicating with them.

- Write one thing for which you will pray daily or weekly for each person.

- Identify the difficulties each person has experienced or is experiencing now.

- Ask God to show you His heart for each person.

Understanding the Lesson

Each lesson has the following three components:

1. **The Invitation: Into the Heart of God.** This component of the lesson preparation and presentation section is designed to invite you, the communicator, and the student into the heart of God, the lesson objective, and the message of the song that accompanies the lesson. This section gives the opportunity for you to search and examine your own heart and consider how the song and the theme address certain things in your own life that God desires to see changed or strengthened. Our ministries are only as strong as our personal devotion to the Lord.

2. **The Impartation: Into the knowledge of God.** This component of the lesson preparation and presentation section will help you understand the Word of God and personally apply the biblical content so you can teach each lesson objective with authority and passion.

3. **The Lesson Presentation Template.** This component will assist you in developing an action plan, and preparing to communicate the lesson in your own words, combining the biblical text and the song. The Lesson Presentation Template includes the following components.

   - **The Invitation:** Invite those you teach to know your heart for them and the lesson you will be teaching. Become transparent and reachable. Communicate your desire that they experience the lesson and the heart and love God has for them.

   - **The Impartation:** Invite those you teach into the knowledge of God through His Word.

   - **The Application: Applying the Truth to Our Lives.** Use the template to prepare your heart and mind for the lesson and to create an action plan for teaching the lesson and communicating the truths the lesson contains.

   - **The Impact: Letting God Have All of Us.** Having done the exercise yourself before teaching, assist and guide the students as they write out action plans that will enable them to apply and communicate what they have learned in the lesson to impact and influence their family, friends, schools, neighborhoods and the nations for God.

LESSON 1: There is Only One God

Biblical Foundation: Book of Job

Song: "Dub the Morning Star"

Objective: For the students to understand that God is fully trustworthy and our response to Him should always be one of praise, no matter what our circumstances may be, for He will always love us. In this lesson, the students will learn the value of loving God with all their strength, which means to love and obey Him, even when they may not feel like it.

Resource Materials Needed:

- *Praise* CD
- Sound system to play the CD
- Handouts of the lyrics to "Dub the Morning Star"
- Your Bible and a Bible for each student
- Your journal and a journal for each student

Praise

I. The Invitation: Into the Heart of God

This step will assist you in preparing to bring the heart of the message together with the heart of the music, while embracing the heart of God for the students you will be teaching.

   A. Listen to "Dub the Morning Star" several times.

   B. As you listen to the song, write in your journal the key phrases and lyrics from the song that impact you the most.

II. The Impartation: Into the Knowledge of God

This step will help you understand why the song was written and identify the main points to communicate about the song. It will also help you gain insight into the biblical foundations of the lesson and the song as you consider the truths contained in the song and study the Word of God.

A. Consider the following:

1. This song was written to communicate the truth that we can praise God no matter what our circumstances may be. As the God of all creation, God is in control of our lives.

2. Praising God helps us keep our eyes off ourselves and our circumstances and on who God is. Sometimes we need to ask ourselves and our students if we know who God is in the midst of crisis, rejection and other painful or hurtful emotions. This song helps us reflect on the beauty of God, which is all around us.

3. This song encourages us to focus on Jesus and our knowledge that He is Lord of our lives, and reminds us that "there is only one God." Even before we were created, God created the earth. This is why we can praise Him with all of our souls and all of our strength.

4. Many people give praise to God only after He answers their prayers or after something goes "well" in their lives. Though these are valuable times of giving thanks to God, this song reminds us that we are to praise Him for who He is, not only for what He does.

B. Read the Book of Job and meditate on chapters 38-42. There are ten key points to communicate about the Book of Job.

1. Job had everything! He had finances, a family and a house with land.

2. In Job 1:7, God asked Satan where Satan came from. Satan answered God's question: "From going to and fro on the earth." It was as if Satan was telling God that the earth was Satan's territory.

3. In Job 1:8, the Lord then asked Satan, "Have you considered My servant Job, there is none like him on the earth, a blameless and upright man, one who fears God and shuns evil?"

Praise

4. The Lord knew Job had a pure heart, but Satan thought Job loved God because of all the possessions Job had.

5. God knew exactly who Job was and what his character was like.

6. The Lord gave Satan permission to attack Job and as a result, Job lost everything.

7. Job's family and friends assumed and told Job that there was no doubt that God held something against him. They insisted he must have done something wrong to deserve his circumstances and they wondered why he didn't just curse God and die.

8. Rather than react as those around him suggested, Job instead chose to pursue a deeper relationship with God. He decided to wrestle with God and ask Him about what was going on. He decided to ask God why these things were happening in order to know God's heart.

9. God answered Job. Read and refer to chapters 38-41.

10. In Job 42, Job responded to God, received blessing and saw his children and grandchildren for four generations.

III. Preparation: Action Plan and Lesson Presentation Template

This step will help you develop an action plan to communicate the lesson using a template. This lesson presentation template has been designed to assist you in organizing the lesson and presenting it in the most effective manner.

Bearing in mind all that you have considered and learned by studying the lesson and contemplating the song, you will now compose the action plan. Again, it is important to remember that the definition of "curriculum" is derived from the Latin term meaning "course of ground."

We teachers are to serve those we teach. They are not to serve us. Remember that we serve them so they will in turn serve God and come to a greater understanding of His ways and His works in their lives. Be sensitive to the needs of the students, keeping in mind that God is faithful and good and knows them best.

"S.E.R.V.A.N.T." Spelled Out

S: "Share" – Share your life with your students.

E: "Example" – Be an example of the truth to your students.

R: "Represent" – Represent Christ correctly to your students.

V: "Voice" – Assist your students in hearing God's voice.

A: "Authority" – Teach in the power of God with His authority.

N: "Needs" – Meet the needs of your students so God is glorified.

T: "Train and Teach" – As you train and teach, do so rightly dividing the Word of God.

Praise

Lesson Presentation Template

Theme: Praise

Lesson: "There is Only One God"

Lesson Biblical Foundation: The Life of Job

Song: "Dub the Morning Star"

PART ONE: The Invitation

In this section, you will invite your students to know your heart for them and the lesson you are teaching. Be transparent and reachable. Communicate your desire that they experience the lesson and the heart and love God has for them.

  A. Play "Dub the Morning Star."

  B. Have the students write down what they think the key points of the song are.

  C. Share your responses to the following questions.

   a. How has studying and reflecting on this lesson changed you?

   b. How can you best explain these changes?

   c. What changes have you made in your own life that you are comfortable sharing?

PART TWO: The Impartation

In this section, you will invite the students into the knowledge of God through His Word.

A. Have the students open their Bibles and read Job 1:6-12.

B. Begin a dialog and ask them to give their thoughts about these six verses. Remember to let them share openly.

C. Communicate at least five points you have identified as being the most important in the Book of Job.

- Point #1:

- Point #2:

- Point #3:

- Point #4:

- Point #5:

D. Ask the students to identify some attributes of the knowledge and character of God that will sustain our hearts in difficult times.

Praise

PART THREE: The Application

In this section, you will help the students identify areas of their lives where they can apply God's Word and His emotions.

Note: They should have their journals with them and be prepared to write in them.

A. Ask the students to identify and write in their journals at least two experiences that caused them to be angry with God. Give them an example.

B. Ask them to identify and write in their journals the things in their lives over which they have control. Give them examples.

C. Ask them to identify and write in their journals the things in their lives over which they have NO control. Give them examples.

D. Ask them to identify and write in their journals what areas in their lives are currently controlling them? Give some examples.

E. Ask them to consider how a relationship with God is meant to sustain and comfort them and help them overcome difficulties and struggles.

PART FOUR: The Impact

A. Explain to your students that God wants all of us. We must learn and practice letting God into all areas of our lives.

B. Play the song again and ask the students to sing along. Give them the lyrics provided in this workbook.

C. Pray the following prayer all together out loud.

God, You sent Your only Son to earth to die for my sins and pay the ultimate price for my transgressions. Today, I give to you my life and ask that you be Lord over my life. No matter what my circumstances might be, I will praise You, God. I will give You thanks. I will sing of Your wonders and all You have done.

God, I rejoice that You are not a mostly mad and sad God, but a glad God. I praise You and I praise Your name. Your name is above all names. You created the heavens and when I am feeling down, I will point to the heavens and say that You are the God of my salvation.

God, break off all depression and let me feel the emotions that You have for me. I close the door to the areas in my life where Satan has had a grip. I ask, God, that through the power of the Holy Spirit, You would give me strength to put all my concerns, hurts and trials into Your hands and trust Jesus as my Savior and Lord. In Jesus' name, amen.

D. Ask if there is anyone who would like individual prayer. Pray for them and ask others to join you in praying for them, when appropriate.

Praise

Student Journal and Notes

_____

_____

_____

_____

_____

_____

_____

_____

_____

_____

_____

_____

_____

_____

LESSON TWO: His Great Love

Biblical Foundation: 1 John 4:19 and Psalm 136

Song: "What's Above"

Objective: For the students to understand and be certain that God's love endures forever. In this lesson, the students will learn that, because of His great love for us, we can respond by offering up our praise to Him.

Resource Materials Needed:

- *Praise* CD
- Sound system to play the CD
- Handouts of the lyrics to "What's Above"
- Your Bible and a Bible for each student
- Your journal and a journal for each student

Praise

I.   The Invitation: Into the Heart of God

This step will assist you in preparing to bring the heart of the message together with the heart of the music, while embracing the heart of God for the students you will be teaching.

    A. Listen to "What's Above" several times.

    B. As you listen to the song, write in your journal the key phrases and lyrics from the song that impact you the most.

II. The Impartation: Into the Knowledge of God

This step will help you understand why the song was written and identify the main points to communicate about the song. It will also help you gain insight into the biblical foundations of the lesson and the song as you consider the truths contained in the song and study the Word of God.

   A. Consider the following:

      1. This song conveys to our hearts and minds that God is a relational God. The lyrics to this song help us reflect on some powerful realities of God's love that we easily forget.

         • "For the first time since the last time I fell in love with You" speaks of the never-ending cycle of falling in love with God when His heart is revealed to us.

         • "I have found what's above" reminds us we need to focus on the Lord.

         • "I hope this never ends" shows the excitement and enjoyment of continually discovering God's love for us.

      2. This song reflects an attitude of abandoned worship as a response to God's love.

      3. This song reminds us that God truly is love and His love endures forever.

   B. Read 1 John 4:19 and Psalm 136. Following are the key points to communicate about these Scriptures.

      1. Psalm 136 is about God's gracious saving power toward Israel. As a reflection of God's loving faithfulness to Israel, it serves as a picture of His unfailing love for us.

      2. The Psalm is about God's steadfast love being the very anchor of His goodness.

      3. This Psalm reveals God's supremacy over all creation.

4. This Psalm reveals the exalted God of heaven. This leads us into praise that is centered around His steadfast love, which endures forever.

5. In 1 John 4:19, John reminded us that our response in love to God comes from knowing the truth that He first loved us.

6. This God, who created the heavens and the earth and all that is in them by just the power of His Word, loves us.

7. Our love originated in our realizing His love for us. Our response of love to God and others is birthed out of the revelation of His love for us.

III. Preparation: Action Plan and Lesson Presentation Template

This step will help you develop an action plan to communicate the lesson using a template. This lesson presentation template has been designed to assist you in organizing the lesson and presenting it in the most effective manner.

Bearing in mind all that you have considered and learned by studying the lesson and contemplating the song, you will now compose the action plan. Again, it is important to remember that the definition of "curriculum" is derived from the Latin term meaning "course of ground."

We teachers are to serve those we teach. They are not to serve us. Remember that we serve them so they will in turn serve God and come to a greater understanding of His ways and His works in their lives. Be sensitive to the needs of the students, keeping in mind that God is faithful and good and knows them best.

"S.E.R.V.A.N.T." Spelled Out

S: "Share" – Share your life with your students.

E: "Example" – Be an example of the truth to your students.

R: "Represent" – Represent Christ correctly to your students.

V: "Voice" – Assist your students in hearing God's voice.

A: "Authority" – Teach in the power of God with His authority.

N: "Needs" – Meet the needs of your students so God is glorified.

T: "Train and Teach" – As you train and teach, do so rightly dividing the Word of God.

Praise

Lesson Presentation Template

Theme: Praise

Lesson: "His Great Love"

Lesson Biblical Foundation: 1 John 4:19 and Psalm 136

Song: "What's Above"

PART ONE: The Invitation

In this section, you will invite your students to know your heart for them and the lesson you are teaching. Be transparent and reachable. Communicate your desire that they experience the lesson and the heart and love God has for them.

    A. Play "What's Above."

    B. Have the students write down what they think the key points of the song are.

    C. Share your responses to the following questions.

        a. What is true love?

        b. How would you define God's steadfast love towards you?

        c. What does loyalty mean to you?

d. What are the most important relationships in your life and why?

e. What changes do you need to make in your own life regarding your understanding of God's love for you that you would be comfortable sharing?

f. Can you think of someone you love and for whom, because of your love, you would sacrifice personal things and even the relationship itself?

g. Correlate the above answer with God's sacrificial love.

Praise

PART TWO: The Impartation

In this section, you will invite the students into the knowledge of God through His Word.

A. Have the students open their Bibles and read 1 John 4:19 and Psalm 136.

B. Communicate at least five points you have identified as being the most important in these Scriptures.

- Point #1:

- Point #2:

- Point #3:

- Point #4:

- Point #5:

C. Ask them to consider, based on the Word of God, how far they think God is willing to go to have a relationship with them.

D. Ask if there is anything that they can think of that would stand in the way of a relationship with the Lord.

PART THREE: The Application

In this section, you will help the students identify areas of their lives where they can apply God's Word and His emotions. Ask the students to write answers to the following questions in their journals.

Note: They should have their journals with them and be prepared to write in them.

    A. How has listening to this song and understanding God's Word impacted you?

    B. Knowing that you are unconditionally loved by God, how will this change the way you will respond to God and others?

    C. In light of God's unconditional love that never fails, how will you have more confidence during life's difficult circumstances?

    D. What are godly characteristics that would define a pure relationship?

    E. How do you personally get close to people?

    F. How can you bring God's unconditional love into relationships with your family, friends, and others?

Praise

PART FOUR: The Impact

A. Explain to your students that God wants all of us. We must learn and practice letting God into all areas of our lives.

B. Play the song again and ask the students to sing along. Give them the lyrics provided in this workbook.

C. Read aloud 1 John 4:19 and Psalm 136 again. Ask the Holy Spirit to reveal to the students any relationships in their lives that need to be strengthened.

D. While in an attitude of prayer, ask if anyone needs to forgive someone.

E. Invite the Holy Spirit to open up their hearts and let the revelation of God's never ending love for them be the foundation for them having pure and holy relationships all the days of their lives.

F. Pray the following prayer all together out loud.

God, You sent Your only Son to earth to die for my sins and pay the ultimate price for my transgressions. For this I thank You. You love me so much! Thank You for wanting to be near me and be with me always. Thank You for creating every unique part of me from the color of my hair to the tiniest freckle on my foot. You knew me before the world began.

Jesus, because You love me this much I want to make a covenant with You. Seal my heart with Your name and I will be Yours always. Nothing can take Your name from my heart. Set this seal on me forever, Jesus. I will always love You. In Jesus' name, amen.

G. Ask if there is anyone who would like individual prayer. Pray for them and ask others to join you in praying for them, when appropriate.

Student Journal and Notes

_____

_____

_____

_____

_____

_____

_____

_____

_____

_____

_____

_____

_____

_____

LESSON THREE: The Choice

Biblical Foundation: Joshua 24:15; 1 Kings 18:21; Psalm 45:10-11

Song: "Every Moment"

Objective: For the students to understand that we have to choose each day to serve God. In this lesson, the students will learn that though there are many influences that impact their lives, they can make a choice to hear God's voice, knowing they belong to Him.

Resource Materials Needed:

- *Praise* CD
- Sound system to play the CD
- Handouts of the lyrics to "Every Moment"
- Your Bible and a Bible for each student
- Your journal and a journal for each student

Praise

I. The Invitation: Into the Heart of God

This step will assist you in preparing to bring the heart of the message together with the heart of the music, while embracing the heart of God for the students you will be teaching.

   A. Listen to "Every Moment" several times.

   B. As you listen to the song, write in your journal the key phrases and lyrics from the song that impact you the most.

II. The Impartation: Into the Knowledge of God

This step will help you understand why the song was written and identify the main points to communicate about the song. It will also help you gain insight into the biblical foundations of the lesson and the song as you consider the truths contained in the song and study the Word of God.

    A. Consider the following:

        1. This song unfolds the drama of how the listener "has a choice to make." Each of us has a choice about whom we will follow and to whom we will listen.

        2. The lyrics, "where do you belong," remind us to choose where and to whom we are going to pledge our allegiance.

        3. The lyrics, "When the world's voice is the only sound," remind us we must choose to praise God; and we must choose Him and His voice in spite of all the other "voices" that surround us.

        4. The lyrics, "Seek Him with all your heart you will find," remind us of God's attainability, regardless of our circumstances. God is near to those who seek Him.

        5. The lyrics, "shake this world off and set my eyes," encourage us to brush off the things of this world and set our focus on God. It again emphasizes our choice.

    B. Read Joshua 24:15; 1 Kings 18:21; and Psalm 45:10-11. Following are the key points to communicate about these Scriptures.

        1. Joshua 24:14 speaks of exclusive loyalty to God, and urges us to put away all other gods and anything else that might stand in the way of our loyalty to God.

        2. Joshua says that, although our fathers (ancestors, others in our families) may have served other gods, we have the opportunity to choose this day whom we will serve. Joshua stated, "as for me and my house, we will serve the Lord."

        3. 1 Kings 18:21 reveals that Elijah made it clear that if Yahweh is your God, follow Him; but if Baal is your god, follow him.

4. It is important to know that Elijah was speaking to a group of people who did not want to reject the worship of Yahweh, they just wanted to include the worship of Baal as well.

5. This text reminds us that worshiping God leaves no room for other gods.

6. Psalm 45:10-11 speaks of a bride who is being exhorted "to consider and incline her ear." God wants her to hear His voice and no others.

7. In the Psalm, the bride is exhorted to forget her own people, and even her father's house, because the King (Jesus) greatly desires her beauty. She is reminded that He is her Lord and that she is to worship Him alone.

8. Christians are the Bride of Christ, and God wants us to hear only His voice and worship only Him.

III. Preparation: Action Plan and Lesson Presentation Template

This step will help you develop an action plan to communicate the lesson using a template. This lesson presentation template has been designed to assist you in organizing the lesson and presenting it in the most effective manner.

Bearing in mind all that you have considered and learned by studying the lesson and contemplating the song, you will now compose the action plan. Again, it is important to remember that the definition of "curriculum" is derived from the Latin term meaning "course of ground."

We teachers are to serve those we teach. They are not to serve us. Remember that we serve them so they will in turn serve God and come to a greater understanding of His ways and His works in their lives. Be sensitive to the needs of the students, keeping in mind that God is faithful and good and knows them best.

"S.E.R.V.A.N.T." Spelled Out

S: "Share" – Share your life with your students.

E: "Example" – Be an example of the truth to your students.

R: "Represent" – Represent Christ correctly to your students.

V: "Voice" – Assist your students in hearing God's voice.

A: "Authority" – Teach in the power of God with His authority.

N: "Needs" – Meet the needs of your students so God is glorified.

T: "Train and Teach" – As you train and teach, do so rightly dividing the Word of God.

Praise

Lesson Presentation Template

Theme: Praise

Lesson: "The Choice"

Lesson Biblical Foundation: Joshua 24:15; 1 Kings 18:21; Psalm 45:10-11

Song: "Every Moment"

PART ONE: The Invitation

In this section, you will invite your students to know your heart for them and the lesson you are teaching. Be transparent and reachable. Communicate your desire that they experience the lesson and the heart and love God has for them.

A. Play "Every Moment."

B. Have the students write down what they think the key points of the song are.

C. Share your responses to the following questions.

   a. List the main relationships in your life. Who influences you the most?

   b. Whose voice stands out among the others and why?

   c. Whose life do you speak into the most?

d. Why is your voice effective in that person's life?

e. Are the voices in your life influencing you to fulfill your destiny in God or are they hindering you from your destiny in God?

f. What have been some of the worst choices you have made and who helped influence them?

g. Have you received bad advice? What was it?

h. In our choices, we choose how we spend our time. How do you spend most of your time? God, friends, family, hobbies, etc.?

i. What changes will you make in your life to make God first?

Praise

PART TWO: The Impartation

In this section, you will invite the students into the knowledge of God through His Word.

    A. Have the students open their Bibles and read Joshua 24:14; 1 Kings 18:21; and Psalm 45:10-11.

    B. Communicate at least five points you have identified as being the most important in these Scriptures.

- Point #1:

- Point #2:

- Point #3:

- Point #4:

- Point #5:

    C. Point out some examples of things that can be obstacles to our relationships with God and/or idols (objects of affection) that we often put before God.

    D. Ask them whom they will allow to be the main voice in their lives? Listen to their responses.

PART THREE: The Application

In this section, you will help the students identify areas of their lives where they can apply God's Word and His emotions. Ask the students to write the answers to the following questions in their journals.

Note: They should have their journals with them and be prepared to write in them.

A. How has listening to this song and understanding God's Word impacted you?

B. Knowing that you are to choose to serve God, what changes will you make regarding relationships and their influence in your life?

C. In light of the command not to serve any other gods, how much more time will you devote to God and your relationship with Him?

D. What decisions are in front of you now and how will this lesson change how you will make those decisions?

Praise

PART FOUR: The Impact

A. Explain to your students that God wants all of us. We must learn and practice letting God into all areas of our lives.

B. Play the song again and ask the students to sing along. Give them the lyrics provided in this workbook.

C. Read aloud 1 Kings 18:21 and invite the Holy Spirit to come. Ask the students to take the results of any past wrong choices to the Cross. Encourage them to repent for putting other voices above God's voice and for any sin that has taken place as a result of these bad choices. Speak of God's forgiveness to help them experience total forgiveness and freedom.

D. In prayer, exhort them to bring before the Lord the difficult choices that are currently facing them. Ask them to invite the power of God into these choices.

E. Pray the following prayer all together out loud.

God, You sent Your only Son to earth to die for my sins and pay the ultimate price for my sins and the poor choices I have made. God, today through Jesus Christ and the power of the Holy Spirit, I ask for Your holy fire to consume me in all my life circumstances. I will choose to serve You this day and I praise You that You know all my circumstances and everything about me.

Father, forgive me for thinking that You are boring and that You don't understand me. Fascinate me as I search for You every day in all my ways. I will love You always and hold true to the revelation of Jesus in my life. In Jesus' name, amen.

F. Ask if there is anyone who would like individual prayer. Pray for them and ask others to join you in praying for them, when appropriate.

Student Journal and Notes

_____

_____

_____

_____

_____

_____

_____

_____

_____

_____

_____

_____

_____

LESSON FOUR: Spontaneous Praise

Biblical Foundation: Psalm 135:1-5 and Psalm 34:1-3

Song: "Atomos"

Objective: To review key aspects of lessons 1-3 and discuss how we can bring praise to God for all that He is. In this lesson, the students will learn the importance of having strong personal relationships with Christ.

Resource Materials Needed:

- *Praise* CD
- Sound system to play the CD
- Your Bible and a Bible for each student
- Your journal and a journal for each student

I. The Invitation: Into the Heart of God

This step will assist you in preparing to bring the heart of the message together with the heart of the music, while embracing the heart of God for the students you will be teaching.

A. Listen to "Atomos" several times.

B. As you listen to the music, write words or describe pictures that God brings to your mind.

II. The Impartation: Into the Knowledge of God

This step will help you understand why the music was written and why the children's prayers were included. It will also help you to identify the main points to communicate about this piece of music. It will also help you gain insight into the biblical foundations of the lesson and the music as you consider the truths contained in the prayer and study the Word of God.

    A. Consider the following:

        1. The song consists of the spontaneous praises of children.

        2. Some of the spontaneous phrases that the children speak are:

- "We praise You for all You have placed on the earth."
- "We praise You for all that You have done."
- "We praise You for how merciful You are."
- "We praise You for Your beauty."
- "You are our treasure."
- "We praise You for being our everlasting Joy."
- "We praise You for always being there."

        3. This song demonstrates how spontaneous we can be in praising God.

    B. Read Psalm 135:1-5 and Psalm 34:1-3. Following are the key points to communicate about these Scriptures.

        1. Psalm 135 has many points of contact with earlier Psalms.

        2. This Psalm was composed for festival and public worship and deliberately designed to evoke memories and associations of other songs of praise.

        3. This Psalm praises God for choosing the Israelites to be His people.

        4. This Psalm is an invitation for the Lord's people to praise Him.

        5. Psalm 34:1-3 communicates the spirit of exuberant confidence we can have in the Lord.

6. In verses 1-2 it is clear that David put his confidence in God and was therefore able to praise God regardless of His circumstances.

7. Psalm 34:3 speaks of magnifying the Lord.

III. Preparation: Action Plan and Lesson Presentation Template

This step will help you develop an action plan to communicate the lesson using a template. This lesson presentation template has been designed to assist you in organizing the lesson and presenting it in the most effective manner.

Bearing in mind all that you have considered and learned by studying the lesson and contemplating the song, you will now compose the action plan. Again, it is important to remember that the definition of "curriculum" is derived from the Latin term meaning "course of ground."

We teachers are to serve those we teach. They are not to serve us. Remember that we serve them so they will in turn serve God and come to a greater understanding of His ways and His works in their lives. Be sensitive to the needs of the students, keeping in mind that God is faithful and good and knows them best.

"S.E.R.V.A.N.T." Spelled Out

S: "Share" – Share your life with your students.

E: "Example" – Be an example of the truth to your students.

R: "Represent" – Represent Christ correctly to your students.

V: "Voice" – Assist your students in hearing God's voice.

A: "Authority" – Teach in the power of God with His authority.

N: "Needs" – Meet the needs of your students so God is glorified.

T: "Train and Teach" – As you train and teach, do so rightly dividing the Word of God.

Praise

Lesson Presentation Template

Theme: Praise

Lesson: "Spontaneous Praise"

Lesson Biblical Foundation: Psalm 135:1-5 and Psalm 34:1-3

Song: "Atomos"

PART ONE: The Invitation

In this section, you will invite your students to know your heart for them and the lesson you are teaching. Be transparent and reachable. Communicate your desire that they experience the lesson and the heart and love God has for them.

    A. Play "Atomos."

    B. Share your responses to the following questions.

        a. Have there been situations in your life that have blessed you, but that you haven't praised God for?

        b. From Lesson 1, what are the key points you remember about Job?

        c. From lesson 2, what are the key points you remember about God's great love?

d. Reflect on recent choices you have made that now glorify the Lord (Lesson 3).

e. Write down everything in your life for which you can give God praise.

Praise

PART TWO: The Impartation

In this section, you will invite the students into the knowledge of God through His Word.

    A. Have the students open their Bibles and read Psalm 135:1-5 and Psalm 34:1-3.

    B. Communicate at least five points you have identified as being the most important in these Scriptures.

- Point #1:

- Point #2:

- Point #3:

- Point #4:

- Point #5:

    C. Write down next to the name of each student any difficult circumstances you know of in their lives. Pray about ways in which you can affirm God in their lives, encourage them, and help them in the midst of the circumstances or even with solutions to the difficult circumstances.

    D. What attributes of God might you share with them or demonstrate to them that would encourage their hearts and bring forth their praise to God?

PART THREE: The Application

In this section, you will help the students identify areas of their lives where they can apply God's Word and His emotions. Ask the students to write answers to the following questions in their journals.

Note: They should have their journals with them and be prepared to write in them.

A. How has listening to the spontaneous praise of the children shown you that you can praise God at all times?

B. During the day how many opportunities do you have to bring praise to God?

C. How can you keep your eyes on Jesus and off yourself and your circumstances?

D. How does God's Word apply to the hardest circumstance or decision that you may have?

Praise

PART FOUR: The Impact

A. Explain to your students that God wants all of us. We must learn and practice letting God into all areas of our lives.

B. Play the first three songs on the *Praise* CD and ask the students to reflect on how they can lift up their praise to the Lord.

C. Play "Atomos" again and encourage the students to sing their own spontaneous song or speak praise to God as it is playing.

D. Pray the following prayer all together out loud.

God, You sent Your only Son to earth to die for my sins and pay the ultimate price to save my life. Lord, I decide today to praise You. Lord, You are the one and only God who can turn my choices into destiny. I will speak of Your great love all the days of my life. I now see that I can praise You any minute of any day for anything. I choose to serve You this day, knowing You have given me the Holy Spirit to help me and guide me through life. In Jesus' name, amen.

E. Ask if there is anyone who would like individual prayer. Pray for them and ask others to join you in praying for them, when appropriate.

Student Journal and Notes

_____

_____

_____

_____

_____

_____

_____

_____

_____

_____

_____

_____

_____

_____

LESSON FIVE: The Father's Heart

Biblical Foundation: Luke 15:11-32

Song: "Dad's Song"

Objective: For the students to understand the Father heart of God. In this lesson, the students will learn about the Father's unconditional love for every person. They will also learn of the forgiveness we have each received from the Father and how we can show forgiveness to others.

Resource Materials Needed:

- *Praise* CD
- Sound system to play the CD
- Handouts of the lyrics to "Dad's Song"
- Your Bible and a Bible for each student
- Your journal and a journal for each student

I.   The Invitation: Into the Heart of God

This step will assist you in preparing to bring the heart of the message together with the heart of the music, while embracing the heart of God for the students you will be teaching.

   A. Listen to "Dad's Song" several times.

   B. As you listen to the song, write in your journal the key phrases and lyrics from the song that impact you the most.

II. The Impartation: Into the Knowledge of God

This step will help you understand why the song was written and identify the main points to communicate about the song. It will also help you gain insight into the biblical foundations of the lesson and the song as you consider the truths contained in the song and study the Word of God.

A. Consider the following:

1. This song originated out of a need for reconciliation with an earthly father.

2. Sometimes our earthly fathers convey a distorted or wrong image of God. This song speaks of our heavenly Father and how He fills in the gaps where an earthly father has disappointed us. This song also speaks of God's forgiveness.

3. This song challenges us to consider our relationship with our earthly father. Often when we reconcile with our earthly fathers, a blessing from the Lord is released in our lives. The lyrics show how critical it is for us to experience God's forgiveness and forgive others in return so that we can enjoy the true blessings of God.

4. This song is meant to bring comfort to those who may not have an earthly father or whose earthly father let them down in some or many ways. Some fathers have left their children to grow up with only their mothers; other fathers were themselves so broken-hearted, hurting or just plain lazy, and never took enough interest in their children's lives.

5. This song is intended to stir us and encourage us to work toward healing the wounds of abandonment that can keep us from releasing total control of our lives to God.

B. Read Luke 15:11-32. Following are the key points to communicate about this Scripture.

1. Keep in mind that the father character in this story represents Father God. In the story, the younger son demanded to receive his portion of his father's estate early, prior to his father's death, when he normally would have received it.

2. The elder son remained at home and the younger son turned his share into cash and departed to enjoy the proceeds away from home and parental control.

3. When the younger son had wasted all his money living an extravagant lifestyle and had been reduced to nothing, his friends deserted him and he was forced to take a job tending to pigs. This was the most menial form of employment he could have found and one that was particularly loathsome to a Jew, whose culture regarded swine as unclean animals.

4. Finding himself in this desperate state of affairs brought him to repentance. He realized that not only was he in a desperate situation, but due to his actions and choices, he was also unworthy to be called His father's son.

5. Knowing he was only fit to be a servant in his father's house, but figuring that was better than tending swine, he prepared to humble himself, return to his father's house and ask to be a servant.

6. Before reaching home, however, his father ran out to greet him. His father had been hoping and looking for his arrival. Before he could even confess, his father welcomed him back into the family and treated him with great honor.

7. The father—without hesitation—called a feast and reinstated the man as his son.

8. This text demonstrates the powerful and glorious truth that God forgives us without hesitation because of the great love He has for us.

III. Preparation: Action Plan and Lesson Presentation Template

This step will help you develop an action plan to communicate the lesson using a template. This lesson presentation template has been designed to assist you in organizing the lesson and presenting it in the most effective manner.

Bearing in mind all that you have considered and learned by studying the lesson and contemplating the song, you will now compose the action plan. Again, it is important to remember that the definition of "curriculum" is derived from the Latin term meaning "course of ground."

We teachers are to serve those we teach. They are not to serve us. Remember that we serve them so they will in turn serve God and come to a greater understanding of His ways and His works in their lives. Be sensitive to the needs of the students, keeping in mind that God is faithful and good and knows them best.

"S.E.R.V.A.N.T." Spelled Out

S: "Share" – Share your life with your students.

E: "Example" – Be an example of the truth to your students.

R: "Represent" – Represent Christ correctly to your students.

V: "Voice" – Assist your students in hearing God's voice.

A: "Authority" – Teach in the power of God with His authority.

N: "Needs" – Meet the needs of your students so God is glorified.

T: "Train and Teach" – As you train and teach, do so rightly dividing the Word of God.

Praise

Lesson Presentation Template

Theme: Praise

Lesson: "The Father's Heart"

Lesson Biblical Foundation: Luke 15:11-32

Song: "Dad's Song"

PART ONE: The Invitation

In this section, you will invite your students to know your heart for them and the lesson you are teaching. Become transparent and reachable. Communicate your desire that they experience the lesson and the heart and love God has for them.

A. Play "Dad's Song."

B. Have the students write down what they think the key points of the song are.

C. Share your responses to the following questions. It is crucial that you be vulnerable to your group at this point.

   a. What was your relationship with your dad like?

   b. If your relationship with your dad was great, give an example of someone you know personally who didn't have the same experience with their dad.

c. How does your relationship with God reflect your relationship with your earthly dad?

d. How does your relationship with your earthly dad affect your relationship with God?

e. Have you ever sinned and repented to God? What did it feel like to experience the embrace and forgiveness of God, knowing you had done wrong but were still loved and forgiven?

Praise

PART TWO: The Impartation

In this section, you will invite the students into the knowledge of God through His Word.

    A. Have the students open their Bibles and read Luke 15:11-32.

    B. Paraphrase the story of the Prodigal Son.

    C. Communicate at least five points you have identified as being the most important in this Scripture.

    • Point #1:

    • Point #2:

    • Point #3:

    • Point #4:

    • Point #5:

    D. Ask the students if they trust their fathers to help them and show them the right ways to live.

    E. Explain the importance of obeying our fathers. Then explain that there are those who may not be able to trust their fathers because they do not keep their promises or because they are not around. Explain that, even if this is true, God is a Father who can be trusted completely.

    F. Explain that God protects them with His strong arms and keeps them safe. Read Psalm 3.

PART THREE: The Application

In this section, you will help the students identify areas of their lives where they can apply God's Word and His emotions.

Note: They should have their journals with them and be prepared to write in them.

A. Ask the students to journal about their fathers. If they do not have a father, ask them to journal about the father in Luke 15:11-32. They might answer such questions as the following: What is your father like? What kinds of things do you enjoy doing with your father? How can you strengthen your relationship with your father? What do you need to forgive your father for?

B. Ask the students how listening to this song impacted them.

C. Ask them how knowing that the Father's love is unconditional changes the way they respond when they sin. Ask if they want to run to God or from God.

D. Ask them to pray and ask God to show them anything in their lives that may be hindering their relationships with God.

Praise

PART FOUR: The Impact

A. Explain to your students that God wants all of us. We must learn and practice letting God into all areas of our lives.

B. Play the song again and ask the students to sing along. Give them the lyrics provided in this workbook.

C. Invite the Holy Spirit to come and impact the hearts of the students. Call out for the Father's love and embrace. Wait on the Lord. Be patient and allow the song to minister to their hearts.

D. Pray the following prayer all together out loud.

God, You sent Your only Son to earth to die for my sins and pay the ultimate price for my transgressions. God, I might not always understand my dad. I might sometimes feel really mad at my dad because he has left or doesn't seem to care about me or disappoints me. But, God, You have promised that You are the father to the fatherless. I count on You to protect me, keep me on the right road, and give me strength. I can't do it all on my own. I need you Abba Father.

Father, forgive me if I have not honored my dad or if I have disobeyed him. Help me to give my father strength by letting him lead me in tough times. In Jesus' name, amen.

E. Ask if there is anyone who would like individual prayer. Pray for them and ask others to join you in praying for them, when appropriate.

Student Journal and Notes

_____

_____

_____

_____

_____

_____

_____

_____

_____

_____

_____

_____

_____

_____

LESSON SIX: Our Merciful Deliverer

Biblical Foundation: Ephesians 2:4 and Micah 4

Song: "Penitent Prayer"

Objective: For the students to understand that God hears our prayers. In this lesson, the students will learn biblical truths that speak of God's mercy and His strength, which when experienced, cause us to have hearts full of praise.

Resource Materials Needed:

- *Praise* CD
- Sound system to play the CD
- Handouts of the lyrics to "Penitent Prayer"
- Your Bible and a Bible for each student
- Your journal and a journal for each student

Praise

I. The Invitation: Into the Heart of God

This step will assist you in preparing to bring the heart of the message together with the heart of the music, while embracing the heart of God for the students you will be teaching.

   A. Listen to "Penitent Prayer" several times.

   B. As you listen to the song, write in your journal the key phrases and lyrics from the song that impact you the most.

II. The Impartation: Into the Knowledge of God

This step will help you understand why the song was written and identify the main points to communicate about the song. It will also help you gain insight into the biblical foundations of the lesson and the song as you consider the truths contained in the song and study the Word of God.

    A. Consider the following:

        1. The lyrics, "Surely you hear my cry," speak of the confidence we can have in the Lord that He hears our prayers, our cries and our heart's desires.

        2. This song reminds us that, even when we feel helpless, Jesus made the ultimate sacrifice for us by His death on the Cross.

        3. The lyrics, "Deliver me," remind us God is a Deliverer.

        4. The lyrics, "Angel of the Lord, the One I adore," refer to Jesus and speak of the hearts of praise we can have for our King.

        5. The lyrics, "Try to tear Him down, He just keeps rising up," remind us that God is undefeatable.

    B. Read Ephesians 2:4 and Micah 4. Following are the key points to communicate about these Scriptures.

        1. The second chapter of Ephesians first describes what life is like for a person who doesn't have a relationship with Christ, for the person untouched by the influence of His Gospel.

        2. This chapter then goes on to talk about the saving grace of God and how we can have life in God through Jesus Christ, and be delivered from death caused by sin.

        3. The chapter speaks of Paul's heart to see the Gospel spread to future generations.

        4. Ephesians 2:1-3 speaks of the risen and exalted One, the One who gives us spiritual lives.

5. Ephesians 2:4 speaks of the rich divine mercy given to us through Jesus that stands in contrast to the sentence of doom passed on a fallen creation and those who don't accept Jesus.

6. Paul focuses specifically on the act of God giving His Son to us that we may experience mercy, love and grace.

7. In Micah, we read that God assured Micah that his prayer would be answered and that his people would be delivered by God's miraculous power and would enjoy all that God had promised.

III. Preparation: Action Plan and Lesson Presentation Template

This step will help you develop an action plan to communicate the lesson using a template. This lesson presentation template has been designed to assist you in organizing the lesson and presenting it in the most effective manner.

Bearing in mind all that you have considered and learned by studying the lesson and contemplating the song, you will now compose the action plan. Again, it is important to remember that the definition of "curriculum" is derived from the Latin term meaning "course of ground."

We teachers are to serve those we teach. They are not to serve us. Remember that we serve them so they will in turn serve God and come to a greater understanding of His ways and His works in their lives. Be sensitive to the needs of the students, keeping in mind that God is faithful and good and knows them best.

"S.E.R.V.A.N.T." Spelled Out

S: "Share" – Share your life with your students.

E: "Example" – Be an example of the truth to your students.

R: "Represent" – Represent Christ correctly to your students.

V: "Voice" – Assist your students in hearing God's voice.

A: "Authority" – Teach in the power of God with His authority.

N: "Needs" – Meet the needs of your students so God is glorified.

T: "Train and Teach" – As you train and teach, do so rightly dividing the Word of God.

Praise

Lesson Presentation Template

Theme: Praise

Lesson: "Our Merciful Deliverer"

Lesson Biblical Foundation: Ephesians 2:4 and Micah 7:15

Song: "Penitent Prayer"

PART ONE: The Invitation

In this section, you will invite your students to know your heart for them and the lesson you are teaching. Be transparent and reachable. Communicate your desire that they experience the lesson and the heart and love God has for them.

A. Play "Penitent Prayer."

B. Have the students write down what they think the key points of the song are.

C. Share your responses to the following questions.

    a. List times in your life when you cried out to God and He answered you.

    b. How have you seen the power of God move in your life?

c. What are some of your unanswered prayers?

d. Where have you seen God's mercy operating in your life and in your family?

e. Name some of the times in your life when God was strong when you were weak.

Praise

PART TWO: The Impartation

In this section, you will invite the students into the knowledge of God through His Word.

    A. Have the students open their Bibles and read Ephesians 2:4 and Micah 7:15.

    B. Communicate at least five points you have identified as being the most important in these Scriptures.

- Point #1:

- Point #2:

- Point #3:

- Point #4:

- Point #5:

    C. Share about promises that have been given to you that you are waiting for God to fulfill.

    D. Think about each student and try to think of times God has revealed His strength in his or her life. If appropriate, you may consider sharing the instances you remember.

PART THREE: The Application

In this section, you will help the students identify areas of their lives where they can apply God's Word and His emotions.

Note: They should have their journals with them and be prepared to write in them.

        A. Ask the students to journal about prayers that have been answered by God.

        B. Ask them to identify areas or situations in their lives that have overwhelmed them and caused them to feel despair.

        C. Ask them to journal about areas or situations in their lives where God has shown His strength and has delivered them.

        D. Ask them to identify any relationships or situations in their lives where they need to receive God's mercy and deliverance.

        E. Ask them to write down prayers that they would like to see answered.

Praise

PART FOUR: The Impact

A. Explain to your students that God wants all of us. We must learn and practice letting God into all areas of our lives.

B. Play the song again and ask the students to sing along. Give them the lyrics provided in this workbook.

C. Invite the Holy Spirit to come and impact the hearts of the students. Call out for the Father's love and embrace. Wait on the Lord. Be patient and let the song minister to the hearts of the students.

D. Pray the following prayer all together out loud.

God, You sent Your only Son to earth to die for my sins and pay the ultimate price for my transgressions. I praise You for the great mercy You have shown me. I praise You because You have delivered me and You will deliver others who are crying out to You. I praise You for all the prayers You have answered. I praise You for the promises You have given me and for the destiny I have in You. I praise You for Your Word and for my family. I long to get closer and closer to You. I love You for Your great ways. Lord, give me a heart of mercy and compassion for those in need. I will serve You all the days of my life. In Jesus' name, amen.

E. Ask if there is anyone who would like individual prayer. Pray for them and ask others to join you in praying for them, when appropriate.

Student Journal and Notes

_____

_____

_____

_____

_____

_____

_____

_____

_____

_____

_____

_____

_____

_____

LESSON SEVEN: Leaning on the Cross

Biblical Foundation: 1 Corinthians 1:18 and 2:2

Song: "Breathe In"

Objective: For the students to understand that, even in the midst of life's injustices, we need to remember where we came from and the price that was paid for our sins by Jesus on the Cross. In this lesson, the students will learn biblical truths that bring a greater awareness of the nature and characteristics of Jesus, especially as they relate to what He did by dying on the Cross.

Resource Materials Needed:

- *Praise* CD
- Sound system to play the CD
- Handouts of the lyrics to "Breathe In"
- Your Bible and a Bible for each student
- Your journal and a journal for each student

Praise

I. The Invitation: Into the Heart of God

This step will assist you in preparing to bring the heart of the message together with the heart of the music, while embracing the heart of God for the students you will be teaching.

   A. Listen to "Breathe In" several times.

   B. As you listen to the song, write in your journal the key phrases and lyrics from the song that impact you the most.

II. The Impartation: Into the Knowledge of God

This step will help you understand why the song was written and identify the main points to communicate about the song. It will also help you gain insight into the biblical foundations of the lesson and the song as you consider the truths contained in the song and study the Word of God.

A. Consider the following:

1. The lyrics speak of the unrest in our world and of the terrible things that can happen in life.

2. This song also reveals how love can be misdirected if we focus on fleshly desires, such as addictions and other destructive practices.

3. The lyrics, "a careful creation of misrepresentation," reveal that no person is a totally accurate reflection of who God is.

4. The song communicates that a person will fall into the trap of having false loves if he or she is living apart from God, with no understanding of the Cross or the Kingdom of God.

5. The song can remind us of other religions, which demonstrate their so-called "love" through hate and violence. In reality, Jesus, on the Cross, paid the ultimate price for our sin, thus showing us what true, pure, perfect love is all about.

6. The song encourages us to take a stand and to breathe in the goodness of the Lord and reminds us there is a Savior – Jesus – who loves us and will receive our love.

7. This song speaks of our having hearts to live in this world and of the strength we need in our day-to-day lives. The lyrics, "My spirit is dry, my soul is weary," are meant to bring the revelation of our need for the everlasting Father of glory and grace.

8. The lyrics, "make me a solider of truth, honor and love," speak of how we need to stand firm in God, love our neighbors and have compassion for the lost.

B. Read 1 Corinthians 1:18 and 2:2. Following are the key points to communicate about these Scriptures.

    1. Paul speaks of how human wisdom is man-centered, not God-centered.

    2. This text teaches that people who are centered on their own needs and fleshly desires cannot see that they are perishing.

    3. The text says that those who are being saved by the Cross are being saved by the very power of God.

    4. 1 Corinthians 2:2 tells us that though Paul may not have had excellent speech or wisdom as he declared the testimony of God, he did have the full knowledge and embrace of Jesus Christ and Him crucified.

    5. Jesus Christ and the power of His crucifixion takes authority over all the injustices and the sin that so easily ensnares us (Hebrews 12:1).

III. Preparation: Action Plan and Lesson Presentation Template

This step will help you develop an action plan to communicate the lesson using a template. This lesson presentation template has been designed to assist you in organizing the lesson and presenting it in the most effective manner.

Bearing in mind all that you have considered and learned by studying the lesson and contemplating the song, you will now compose the action plan. Again, it is important to remember that the definition of "curriculum" is derived from the Latin term meaning "course of ground."

We teachers are to serve those we teach. They are not to serve us. Remember that we serve them so they will in turn serve God and come to a greater understanding of His ways and His works in their lives. Be sensitive to the needs of the students, keeping in mind that God is faithful and good and knows them best.

"S.E.R.V.A.N.T." Spelled Out

S: "Share" – Share your life with your students.

E: "Example" – Be an example of the truth to your students.

R: "Represent" – Represent Christ correctly to your students.

V: "Voice" – Assist your students in hearing God's voice.

A: "Authority" – Teach in the power of God with His authority.

N: "Needs" – Meet the needs of your students so God is glorified.

T: "Train and Teach" – As you train and teach, do so rightly dividing the Word of God.

Praise

Lesson Presentation Template

Theme: Praise

Lesson: "Leaning on the Cross"

Lesson Biblical Foundation: 1 Corinthians 1:18 and 2:2

Song: "Breathe In"

PART ONE: The Invitation

In this section, you will invite your students to know your heart for them and the lesson you are teaching. Be transparent and reachable. Communicate your desire that they experience the lesson and the heart and love God has for them.

A. Play "Breathe In."

B. Have the students write down what they think the key points of the song are.

C. Share your responses to the following questions.

   a. What injustices do you see on the earth today? How does the message of the Cross enable you to stand in the midst of injustices.

   b. What would the reactions of those around you be if you were to preach the message of the Cross to them?

c. Do you know people in your life right now who are perishing?

d. Do you know people right now serving God in the midst of crises? Who are they and what are their testimonies?

e. What do you think causes people place a high value on false love, false religions, addictions, etc.?

Praise

PART TWO: The Impartation

In this section, you will invite the students into the knowledge of God through His Word.

    A. Have the students open their Bibles and read 1 Corinthians 1:18 and 2:2.

    B. Communicate at least five points you have identified as being the most important in these Scriptures.

- Point #1:

- Point #2:

- Point #3:

- Point #4:

- Point #5:

    C. Think about each student and reflect on where you know God has revealed His strength to them.

    D. Identify areas in your own life in which God has shown His mercy and strength and share this with the students. Explain to them that, because of the Cross, you and they have the power to overcome.

PART THREE: The Application

In this section, you will help the students identify areas of their lives where they can apply God's Word and His emotions.

Note: They should have their journals with them and be prepared to write in them.

        A. Ask the students to journal about areas of their lives that they need to take to Jesus and the Cross.

        B. Ask them to identify situations or circumstances that they feel are not fair.

        C. Ask them to identify false loves and why people serve false gods.

        D. Ask them to identify how they will keep their focus on Christ crucified.

        E. Ask them what "Love your neighbor" means to them and how they could show compassion to others who are in the midst of crises, turmoil, pain, suffering, etc.

Praise

PART FOUR: The Impact

A. Explain to your students that God wants all of us. We must learn and practice letting God into all areas of our lives.

B. Play the song again and ask the students to sing along. Give them the lyrics provided in this workbook. Sing together "Your love extends to the heavens, up into the clouds."

C. Pray the following prayer all together out loud.

God, You sent Your only Son to earth to die for my sins and pay the ultimate price for my transgressions. I praise You for the great mercy You have shown me because of Christ crucified on the Cross. I praise You because You will give me power through the Cross.

I ask that You extend Your power to this earth and to all those who are experiencing crises and are gripped with addictions and false loves. It is because of Your power that I praise You and ask that the Holy Spirit remove all the obstacles in my life where I have not put You first. Give me Your fire to preach the message of the Cross of Jesus with passion, authority and love. In Jesus' name, amen.

D. Ask if there is anyone who would like individual prayer. Pray for them and ask others to join you in praying for them, when appropriate.

Student Journal and Notes

_____

_____

_____

_____

_____

_____

_____

_____

_____

_____

_____

_____

_____

_____

LESSON EIGHT: My Redeemer

Biblical Foundation: Psalm 40:1-3

Song: "The Redeem Theme"

Objective: For the students to understand that God is our Redeemer. In this lesson, the students will learn biblical truths about God being sufficient enough to rescue us and put our feet firmly on the rock of salvation.

Resource Materials Needed:

- *Praise* CD
- Sound system to play the CD
- Handouts of the lyrics to "The Redeem Theme"
- Your Bible and a Bible for each student
- Your journal and a journal for each student

Praise

I.   The Invitation: Into the Heart of God

This step will assist you in preparing to bring the heart of the message together with the heart of the music, while embracing the heart of God for the students you will be teaching.

A. Listen to "The Redeem Theme" several times.

B. As you listen to the song, write in your journal the key phrases and lyrics from the song that impact you the most.

II. The Impartation: Into the Knowledge of God

This step will help you understand why the song was written and identify the main points to communicate about the song. It will also help you gain insight into the biblical foundations of the lesson and the song as you consider the truths contained in the song and study the Word of God.

A. Consider the following:

1. This song speaks of the testimony we have in Jesus.

2. The lyrics, "the life I used to call my own," speak of how we can be amazed of what Jesus has done in our lives.

3. This song speaks of how the Lord has rescued us from miserable situations.

4. The lyrics, "Yeah my Redeemer," remind us to focus on Jesus.

5. This song is meant to be an encouragement to us because, though we are at times out of control, Jesus' love for us never changes.

B. Read Psalm 40:1-3. Following are the key points to communicate about this Scripture.

1. This Psalm shows David's patience while He was waiting upon the Lord.

2. David found comfort in knowing that God had inclined His ear to him and heard his cry. The text speaks of the Lord's ear being alert to David's prayer.

3. Verse 2 speaks of God bringing David out of a place of hopelessness and insecurity, a place the Scripture likens to a horrible pit.

4. David was brought out of the miry clay and his feet were set upon a rock. Verse 2 speaks of how God wants to establish our steps.

5. Verse 3 is a testimony of how God's redeeming power can bring us out of a pit. It is He who puts a new song in our mouths, causing us to continually praise Him.

Praise

III. Preparation: Action Plan and Lesson Presentation Template

This step will help you develop an action plan to communicate the lesson using a template. This lesson presentation template has been designed to assist you in organizing the lesson and presenting it in the most effective manner.

Bearing in mind all that you have considered and learned by studying the lesson and contemplating the song, you will now compose the action plan. Again, it is important to remember that the definition of "curriculum" is derived from the Latin term meaning "course of ground."

We teachers are to serve those we teach. They are not to serve us. Remember that we serve them so they will in turn serve God and come to a greater understanding of His ways and His works in their lives. Be sensitive to the needs of the students, keeping in mind that God is faithful and good and knows them best.

"S.E.R.V.A.N.T." Spelled Out

S: "Share" – Share your life with your students.

E: "Example" – Be an example of the truth to your students.

R: "Represent" – Represent Christ correctly to your students.

V: "Voice" – Assist your students in hearing God's voice.

A: "Authority" – Teach in the power of God with His authority.

N: "Needs" – Meet the needs of your students so God is glorified.

T: "Train and Teach" – As you train and teach, do so rightly dividing the Word of God.

Lesson Presentation Template

Theme: Praise

Lesson: "My Redeemer"

Lesson Biblical Foundation: Psalm 40:1-3

Song: "The Redeem Theme"

PART ONE: The Invitation

In this section, you will invite your students to know your heart for them and the lesson you are teaching. Be transparent and reachable. Communicate your desire that they experience the lesson and the heart and love God has for them.

A. Play "The Redeem Theme."

B. Have the students write down what they think the key points of the song are.

C. Share your responses to the following questions.

  a. List some times you felt you were in a pit.

  b. List some times you have known God's redeeming love.

  c. List some times or situations when you put your trust in yourself, rather than in God.

d. Would you consider yourself to be a patient person? List some times when you might have gotten ahead of God.

e. List some times or situations when you did wait on the Lord and He answered you. Express to the students the joy you felt in those times.

PART TWO: The Impartation

In this section, you will invite the students into the knowledge of God through His Word.

A. Have the students open their Bibles and read Psalm 40:1-3.

B. Communicate at least five points you have identified as being the most important in this Scripture.

- Point #1:

- Point #2:

- Point #3:

- Point #4:

- Point #5:

C. Think about each student and identify area(s) in their lives in which they may feel they are in a "pit."

D. Think about how you can help them be patient in circumstances that are troubling them.

Praise

PART THREE: The Application

In this section, you will help the students identify areas of their lives where they can apply God's Word and His emotions.

Note: They should have their journals with them and be prepared to write in them.

A. Ask the students to journal their positive experiences with being patient and waiting on the Lord.

B. Ask them to identify times in their lives when they handled things on their own without praying or asking for God's guidance and wisdom.

C. Ask them to write down what they think it means to wait on the Lord. You can give examples, such as praying or reading the Bible.

D. Ask them to write their testimony of how they came to know the Lord.

E. Ask them to journal their thoughts on how close they feel to the Lord.

F. Ask them to identify things they could do to become closer to the Lord.

PART FOUR: The Impact

A. Explain to your students that God wants all of us. We must learn and practice letting God into all areas of our lives.

B. Invite the Holy Spirit to come and impact the hearts of the students. Call out for the Father's love and embrace. Play the song. Wait on the Lord. Let the song minister to the hearts of the students.

C. Play the song again and ask the students to sing along. Give them the lyrics provided in this workbook.

D. Pray the following prayer all together out loud.

God, You sent Your only Son to earth to die for my sins and pay the ultimate price for my transgressions. I praise You for the great mercy You have shown me. I praise You because You have brought me out of the miry clay. I praise You because You are my Redeemer and You have delivered me from the horrible pit. I want to thank You that You can establish my steps upon the Rock, which is Jesus. I praise You because You can put a new song in my mouth and many will see it and put their trust in You. I praise You that You have filled my empty soul and I praise You that there is no stopping this awesome feeling that I can experience when I reflect on what Jesus has done for me. In Jesus' name, amen.

E. Ask if there is anyone who would like individual prayer. Pray for them and ask others to join you in praying for them, when appropriate.

Student Journal and Notes

_____

_____

_____

_____

_____

_____

_____

_____

_____

_____

_____

_____

_____

_____

LESSON NINE: Worthy is the Lamb

Biblical Foundation: John 1:29 and Isaiah 53:7

Song: "Beginning"

Objective: For the students to understand that God is worthy of our praise. In this lesson, the students will learn biblical truths that focus on Jesus as the Lamb of God, who takes away the sin of the world.

Resource Materials Needed:

- *Praise* CD
- Sound system to play the CD
- Handouts of the lyrics to "Beginning"
- Your Bible and a Bible for each student
- Your journal and a journal for each student

Praise

I.   The Invitation: Into the Heart of God

This step will assist you in preparing to bring the heart of the message together with the heart of the music, while embracing the heart of God for the students you will be teaching.

    A. Listen to "Beginning" several times.

    B. As you listen to the song, write in your journal the key phrases and lyrics from the song that impact you the most.

II. The Impartation: Into the Knowledge of God

This step will help you understand why the song was written and identify the main points to communicate about the song. It will also help you gain insight into the biblical foundations of the lesson and the song as you consider the truths contained in the song and study the Word of God.

A. Consider the following:

1. This song is a worshipful meditation on the worthiness and holiness of God.

2. The lyrics, "Who was and is to come," remind us that this slain Lamb (Jesus), who took away the sin of the world, will return.

3. The lyrics, "Honor to the Lamb," remind us to honor Jesus in all we do.

B. Read John 1:29 and Isaiah 53:7. Following are the key points to communicate about these Scriptures.

1. John 1:29 describes John's first personal introduction of Jesus to his followers.

2. Jewish minds would relate to the concept of "the Lamb" because lambs were offered as sacrifices in the temple. In fact, sacrificial lambs were so familiar to Jewish minds that it would be difficult for them to think of the concept of the "Lamb of God" in any other context.

3. By saying, "Behold the Lamb of God," John intended for his hearers to understand that Jesus would be the ultimate sacrifice for the forgiveness of sin.

4. Isaiah 53:7 speaks of Jesus' humility as He was led to His death on the Cross just as a lamb would be led to his slaughter.

5. "As a sheep before its shearers, is silent" Jesus opened not His mouth. This speaks of Jesus' humility and utter confidence in His mission to provide salvation for the entire world.

Praise

III. Preparation: Action Plan and Lesson Presentation Template

This step will help you develop an action plan to communicate the lesson using a template. This lesson presentation template has been designed to assist you in organizing the lesson and presenting it in the most effective manner.

Bearing in mind all that you have considered and learned by studying the lesson and contemplating the song, you will now compose the action plan. Again, it is important to remember that the definition of "curriculum" is derived from the Latin term meaning "course of ground."

We teachers are to serve those we teach. They are not to serve us. Remember that we serve them so they will in turn serve God and come to a greater understanding of His ways and His works in their lives. Be sensitive to the needs of the students, keeping in mind that God is faithful and good and knows them best.

"S.E.R.V.A.N.T." Spelled Out

S: "Share" – Share your life with your students.

E: "Example" – Be an example of the truth to your students.

R: "Represent" – Represent Christ correctly to your students.

V: "Voice" – Assist your students in hearing God's voice.

A: "Authority" – Teach in the power of God with His authority.

N: "Needs" – Meet the needs of your students so God is glorified.

T: "Train and Teach" – As you train and teach, do so rightly dividing the Word of God.

Lesson Presentation Template

Theme: Praise

Lesson: "Worthy is the Lamb"

Lesson Biblical Foundation: John 1:29 and Isaiah 53:7

Song: "Beginning"

PART ONE: The Invitation

In this section, you will invite your students to know your heart for them and the lesson you are teaching. Be transparent and reachable. Communicate your desire that they experience the lesson and the heart and love God has for them.

A. Play "Beginning."

B. Have the students write down what they think the key points of the song are.

C. Share your responses to the following questions.

    a. What are some emotions you have when you think about how Jesus went to the Cross without defending Himself to die for your sins?

    b. How can you help the students understand the humility of Jesus?

    c. What does it mean to be found worthy?

d. Have you ever loved and cared about someone so much that you would be willing to give up or sacrifice your most treasured possession for a relationship with them?

e. In what areas of your life do you feel unworthy?

f. How does reading about how Jesus was silent before His accusers challenge you?

g. Have you ever been silent when falsely accused? If so, when?

h. Correlate the above answer with God's sacrificial love.

PART TWO: The Impartation

In this section, you will invite the students into the knowledge of God through His Word.

A. Have the students open their Bibles and read John 1:19 and Isaiah 53:7.

B. Communicate at least five points you have identified as being the most important in these Scriptures.

- Point #1:

- Point #2:

- Point #3:

- Point #4:

- Point #5:

C. Discuss with the students why you were impacted by these verses.

D. Share how you've personalized these verses in your own life.

Praise

PART THREE: The Application

In this section, you will help the students identify areas of their lives where they can apply God's Word and His emotions.

Note: They should have their journals with them and be prepared to write in them.

A. Ask the students to reflect and journal about why Jesus is worthy of our praise.

B. Ask the students to write about times or ways in which they have felt or feel unworthy.

C. Ask them to journal experiences in their lives when they were falsely accused.

D. Ask them to consider how their love for Christ can be strengthened by considering the Scriptures they just read.

E. Ask them to reflect on and journal about how Jesus died for their sins and how understanding the full meaning of what Jesus did might help them become more like Him. Give some examples.

PART FOUR: The Impact

A. Explain to your students that God wants all of us. We must learn and practice letting God into all areas of our lives.

B. Invite the Holy Spirit to come and impact the hearts of the students. Call out for the Father's love and embrace. Play the song. Wait on the Lord and let the song minister to the hearts of the students.

C. Play the song again and ask the students to sing along. Give them the lyrics provided in this workbook.

D. Pray the following prayer all together out loud.

God, You sent Your only Son to earth to die for my sins and pay the ultimate price for my transgressions. Thank You for being completely different than the world. I lift up my praise to You because You were willing to lay down Your life so I may live eternally with You. I will praise You because You are worthy of my love and affection. I praise You for Your humility in embracing the Father's plan. Lord, I want to be more like You! Seal my heart with Your name and I will be Yours always. Nothing can take You from my heart. Set a seal on me forever, Jesus. I will always love you. In Jesus' name, amen.

E. Ask if there is anyone who would like individual prayer. Pray for them and ask others to join you in praying for them, when appropriate.

Praise

Student Journal and Notes

_____

_____

_____

_____

_____

_____

_____

_____

_____

_____

_____

_____

_____

_____

LESSON TEN: The Joy of My Salvation

Biblical Foundation: Habakkuk 3:17-19

Song: "I Will Joy"

Objective: For the students to understand that God is the joy of our salvation. In this lesson, the students will learn biblical truths that will tie in all the Scriptures used in this manual.

Resource Materials Needed:

- *Praise* CD
- Sound system to play the CD
- Handouts of the lyrics to "I Will Joy"
- Your Bible and a Bible for each student
- Your journal and a journal for each student

Praise

I.   The Invitation: Into the Heart of God

This step will assist you in preparing to bring the heart of the message together with the heart of the music, while embracing the heart of God for the students you will be teaching.

    A. Listen to "I Will Joy" several times.

    B. As you listen to the song, write in your journal the key phrases and lyrics from the song that impact you the most.

II. The Impartation: Into the Knowledge of God

This step will help you understand why the song was written and identify the main points to communicate about the song. It will also help you gain insight into the biblical foundations of the lesson and the song as you consider the truths contained in the song and study the Word of God.

A. Consider the following:

1. The lyrics, "Even when the blossom's not on the vine, I will raise my voice," remind us to praise God even when circumstances are not as we would like them to be.

2. The lyrics, "when you come to claim this earth," remind us that God has a divine plan to bring forth righteousness in the earth and for this we can praise Him.

3. This song describes a determined heart that will praise God for His salvation.

4. This song serves as a summary to all the songs on the *Praise* CD.

B. Read Habakkuk 3:17-19. Following are the key points to communicate about this Scripture.

1. The prophet Habakkuk stated his confidence in the Lord in the midst of all other things failing. He did not put his hope in man, but placed his hope and confidence in God and His unchanging character alone.

2. "I will rejoice in the Lord." This text is about personal faith in God.

3. "Though the fig tree does not blossom" references a time when the nation of Judah, whose people gained most of their sustenance from crops such as those listed in the text, had no crops.

4. Realizing the crop sources may fail, Habakkuk affirmed that his existence was not based on the crops alone, but on God. God is the source of all things.

5. Rejoicing sprang from Habakkuk's relationship with God. He knew he could not be deprived of his relationship with God, no matter what else happened or what circumstances he faced.

6. Intimacy with God is a sure foundation. God's promises and unchanging character give us confidence of and in our eternal relationship with God.

7. Habakkuk's confidence and strength lay in the revelation of the lordship of God and in His power.

8. Habakkuk confidently put his faith in the character of God and trusted Him. He relied upon God's promises as a covenant-keeping God.

III. Preparation: Action Plan and Lesson Presentation Template

This step will help you develop an action plan to communicate the lesson using a template. This lesson presentation template has been designed to assist you in organizing the lesson and presenting it in the most effective manner.

Bearing in mind all that you have considered and learned by studying the lesson and contemplating the song, you will now compose the action plan. Again, it is important to remember that the definition of "curriculum" is derived from the Latin term meaning "course of ground."

We teachers are to serve those we teach. They are not to serve us. Remember that we serve them so they will in turn serve God and come to a greater understanding of His ways and His works in their lives. Be sensitive to the needs of the students, keeping in mind that God is faithful and good and knows them best.

"S.E.R.V.A.N.T." Spelled Out

S: "Share" – Share your life with your students.

E: "Example" – Be an example of the truth to your students.

R: "Represent" – Represent Christ correctly to your students.

V: "Voice" – Assist your students in hearing God's voice.

A: "Authority" – Teach in the power of God with His authority.

N: "Needs" – Meet the needs of your students so God is glorified.

T: "Train and Teach" – As you train and teach, do so rightly dividing the Word of God.

Praise

Lesson Presentation Template

Theme: Praise

Lesson: "The Joy of My Salvation"

Lesson Biblical Foundation: Habakkuk 3:17-19

Song: "I Will Joy"

PART ONE: The Invitation

In this section, you will invite your students to know your heart for them and the lesson you are teaching. Be transparent and reachable. Communicate your desire that they experience the lesson and the heart and love God has for them.

    A. Play "I Will Joy."

    B. Have the students write down what they think the key points of the song are.

    C. Share your responses to the following questions.

        a. Think of a difficult time in your life. How did your relationship with the Lord serve as your foundation for having the confidence to make it through that difficult time?

        b. What are some attributes of God that give you strength and courage to lift your voice to the Lord and rejoice in your salvation, even when things are disappointing?

c. Do you believe it is possible to have joy in difficult circumstances? Why or why not?

d. Think of God's unchanging love and His covenant promises to you. How does this make your heart rejoice?

e. Express the joy you feel knowing you cannot be deprived of your relationship with God, no matter your circumstances.

Praise

PART TWO: The Impartation

In this section, you will invite the students into the knowledge of God through His Word.

A. Have the students open their Bibles and read Habakkuk 3:17-19.

B. Communicate at least five points you have identified as being the most important in this Scripture.

- Point #1:

- Point #2:

- Point #3:

- Point #4:

- Point #5:

C. Ask them to identify areas in their lives or situations where they have found it difficult to trust God.

D. Review the Scripture and point out the principle of how we can rejoice in the Lord even when circumstances and people fail us.

PART THREE: The Application

In this section, you will help the students identify areas of their lives where they can apply God's Word and His emotions.

Note: They should have their journals with them and be prepared to write in them.

   A. Ask the students to journal about what it means to rejoice in the Lord for their salvation.

   B. Ask them to write down as many attributes of God as they can for which they can praise Him.

   C. Ask them to apply one attribute from the above list to a disappointing or hard situation they have encountered. Ask them how they can rejoice in it because of who God is.

   D. Ask them to journal their thoughts about knowing that, in spite of everything else, nothing can separate them from the love of God.

   E. Ask them to journal about ways they can develop a stronger relationship with Jesus.

PART FOUR: The Impact

A. Explain to your students that God wants all of us. We must learn and practice letting God into all areas of our lives.

B. Invite the Holy Spirit to come and impact the hearts of the students. Call out for the Father's love and embrace. Play the song. Wait on the Lord and let the song minister to the hearts of the students.

C. Play the song again and ask the students to sing along. Give them the lyrics provided in this workbook.

D. Pray the following prayer all together out loud.

God, You sent Your only Son to earth to die for my sins and pay the ultimate price for my transgressions. For this I thank You with all that I am. You love me so much! Thank You for wanting to be near me and be with me always. I praise You because nothing can separate me from my relationship with You. I praise You because Your character is never changing. I praise You because I can trust You and Your promises never fail me.

I praise You because You have set Your love on me and I choose this day to lift my voice in praise to You for Your salvation. I praise You for Your great love that never changes and never fails me. I praise You for being my source for all things. I praise You for who You are.

Seal my heart with Your name and I will be Yours always. Nothing can take You from my heart. Set this seal on me forever, Jesus. I will lift my voice in worship to You for who You are in all my circumstances. In Jesus' name, amen.

E. Ask if there is anyone who would like individual prayer. Pray for them and ask others to join you in praying for them, when appropriate.

Student Journal and Notes

_____

_____

_____

_____

_____

_____

_____

_____

_____

_____

_____

_____

_____

_____

Song Lyrics

Praise

Dub the Morning Star

Long before I knew you Father
You showed the sun its place
While the stars all sang together
You gave the earth its face

And when my heart / Says "why"
I'll talk to the seas / And they'll cry

Whoah (4x)
There is only one God
Praise the Lord O my soul (2x)

I can see all Your footprints / Your light shines every place
The trees are Your artwork / The skies speak of Your grace

And when my heart / Says "why"
I'll talk to the seas / And they'll cry

Whoah (4x)
There is only one God
Praise the Lord O my soul (2x)

What's Above

Here I am / Seeing You
For the first time since the last time
I fell in love with You; again
And I hope this never ends
I hope this never ends

'Cause what I've found / Is what's above
I never thought it could be so simple but
Who can deny that You and I are desperately in love
Desperately in love (2x)

There's only One / That I'm
Living for / This time around and now
We've reached the edge / And I hope we jump off it
And start this all again

'Cause what I've found / Is what's above
I never thought it could be so simple but
Who can deny that You and I are desperately in love
Desperately in love (2x)

I know your pain / I sense your fears
But there's only one way / DOWNNNN

'Cause what I've found / Is what's above
I never thought it could be so simple but
Who can deny that You and I are desperately in love
Desperately in love (2x)

Every Moment

We've got a choice to make
Or something's going to break
Stop and look around
"Where do you belong"
When the world's voice is the only sound
Remember that
If you seek Him with all your heart
You will find (3x)
His presence / The Savior
Is what we came for
Every moment I wake I wait for You
Every step that I take I walk towards You (2x)

Choose for yourself / whom you will
Whom you will serve
From this day on / and always and always
You are my Lord
You are my cry
Shake this world off
And set my eyes
One look / one sigh
I'm there / oh yes I'll find

Atomos

Every moment...
Every moment...

Dad's Song

Hello my friend
It's good to hear You again
Even though I can't see / I still believe
That You're right here / Even though I fear
I've let it go between us / I just don't feel worthy

But like a father to a son / Even though wrong's been done
You've reached out Your arms and welcomed me
So now my heart sings / We forget all these things
And I fall to my knees / Your majesty

There's nothing I'd rather do
Than spend my whole life with You
There's only room for You inside
Only one place to confide
We'll go from sea to sea / Your grace to carry me
But what if I don't defend / And fail You again

But like a father to a son / Even though wrong's been done
You've reached out Your arms and welcomed me
So now my heart sings / We forget all these things
And I fall to my knees / Your majesty

I'm calling out to You (2x)
Calling out to You Lord, I'm calling out to You Lord
I'm calling out / Calling out to You

But like a father to a son / Even though wrong's been done
You've reached out Your arms and welcomed me
So now my heart sings / We forget all these things
And I fall to my knees / Your majesty

The Penitent Prayer

Mercy
Surely You hear my cry
Deliver me / Before the sun sets on my life
Emmanuel / I try I try
To do it all solely / No man can be
His own army / You are my own
My only hope is in You

Angel of the Lord / The One whom I adore
You are my hiding place
I have to see Your face (2x)

Mercy
Surely You hear my cry
Deliver me / Before the sun sets on my life
Emmanuel / I try I try
To do it all solely / No man can be
His own army / You are my own
My only hope is in You

Angel of the Lord / The One whom I adore
You are my hiding place
I have to see Your face (2x)

Holy Ghost of heaven / You are my fortress
My fortress / Try to tear Him down
He just keeps rising up / Holy Ghost of heaven
Of heaven
Glory to You (2x)

Breathe In

Breathe in now / Breathe in
Breathe out (4x)

Stress, stress, stress / I'm in such unrest
Is this a dream or am I really seeing this mess
War crimes and hate crimes and blood signs
Hustling up the streets without a moment to realize
A careful creation of misrepresentation
The author of sin who's taking my nation
Don't forget who you are or forget where you came from

The heavenly Ghost of the clouds and His kingdom
It's a reason to rise and open your eyes and see
All the good God's done / His Spirit within me
So get up, stand up, / Raise your hands up
And tell the only One He's done much more
Than a bang up / Your love extends to the heavens
Up into the clouds / You're faithful unto the heavens
But have compassion as You have, my Savior

I love You /
I love You Lord (2x)

Breathe in now / Breathe in
Breathe out (4x)

Everlasting Father of Glory and Grace
Give me a hint and a heart to live in this place
My spirit is dry / My soul is weary
Hack through my darkness so I can see clearly
Make me a soldier of truth, honor and love
So I can stand firm and put on my gloves
Set me not to destroy and tear down my neighbor
But have compassion as You had, my Savior

Your Love... (2x)

The Redeem Theme

When I look back
On the life that I used to call my own
I can't believe He…
He brought me through my life so miserable
Jesus Jesus Jesus Jesus Jesus Jesus
Yeah, My Redeemer (8x)
Try to stop me / I'm electric
He's filled my empty soul / There's no stopping
This awesome feeling / I've lost all control
To
Jesus Jesus Jesus Jesus Jesus Jesus Yeah
My Redeemer (8x)

Beginning

Worthy, worthy is the Lamb
Honor, honor to the Lamb

Holy, Holy is the Lord God Almighty
Who was and is to come (2x)
Who is…

Worthy, worthy is the Lamb
Honor, honor to the Lamb

Holy, Holy is the Lord God Almighty
Who was and is to come (2x)
Who is…

I Will Joy

Even when the blossom's not on the vine
I will raise my voice / To You O Lord Divine
The joy of the Lord is my Salvation

Even when…
The deep…
Even when…

The deep uttered its voice / And lifted its hands on high
The sun and moon inhabit / The light of Your eyes
And when I've lost my way
I will lift my head up to You and say

© 2005 Dustin Frank/Forerunner Music

Age Group Characteristics and Communication Tips

I.   Basic Age Group Characteristics to remember when adapting a lesson to be age group appropriate.

   A.   8-Year-Olds

      1.   They may spread themselves too thin and things may wind up in a mess.

      2.   Relationships between parents and children may get complicated.

      3.   They fair well with other siblings.

      4.   School is important because friends are there.

      5.   About God...Children should learn that God is all powerful, all knowing, is everywhere, is with them at all times, loves them and wants to have a relationship with them.

    a. God wants them to know that each of them is special in His sight. God cares for and loves their families too.

    b. God wants them to talk with Him in prayer every day.

    c. God always answers prayer with "yes" or "no" or "wait." He provides all they need. He can be trusted for all things.

6.   About Jesus...Children should learn that Jesus is the Son of God who came to Earth to be our Savior and die for our sins.

    a. Jesus wants all people to come to Him as their Lord and Savior. Jesus is the only way to God and Heaven.

    b. Jesus wants to take sins from our lives. Jesus was perfect and never did anything wrong.

    c. Jesus rose from the dead and now lives in Heaven. He is preparing a place for us to live with Him in Heaven.

    d. Jesus will return some day to take us home forever. He loves us and is our best friend. Jesus wants us to love and obey Him and do the things that He taught us to do.

7.   About the Holy Spirit...Children should learn that when Jesus went to Heaven He sent the Holy Spirit as our comforter and teacher.

    a. The Holy Spirit will give us the power and desire to do the will of the Father.

    b. Through the Holy Spirit we can participate in the things that Jesus did and told us to do.

    c. The Holy Spirit will speak to our hearts and show us where there is sin.

    d. He will help us worship the Lord and give us things to say to the Lord.

e. It is through the work of the Holy Spirit that we will see healing, miracles and changed lives.

f. Through the power of the Holy Spirit others will come to know Jesus.

8. About the Bible...Children should learn that it is God's Word to His children.

a. The Bible tells us what God wants and how we are to live our lives in relationship with Him.

b. The Bible reveals God's perfect love for us. It tells us about how He related to other people. It tells us about who we are and why we were created.

c. The Bible has two major parts called the Old Testament and the New Testament. There are sixty-six books in the Bible.

d. We should read and memorize it so that we will be built up and strengthened by God's Word to us.

9. About home and parents...Parents have rules for them to follow but God also has rules for them to follow.

a. God wants to be at home in their household and to be in authority there.

b. God wants to restore their home when there is sin present.

c. They can go to the Father in prayer to receive help and restoration for their homes and for their relationships.

d. They can be ambassadors in their homes to any non-believers living there.

10. About church...Children should learn that they come to church to learn about God, Jesus and the Holy Spirit.

a. Church is a place to see friends and enjoy others. It is a place where they can feel loved, warm and safe.

b. Church is a place where other people really show their love and care.

c. Church is God's house and is a place where we come to worship God and pray for one another.

d. Church is more than a building; it is also the people who make up the church.

e. They can give money to the church to help buy things and provide outreach to others.

11. About others...Children should learn that God loves all people and He wants them to show love and compassion for others.

a. God wants them to lead others to Jesus in love and in deed. He wants them to pray for others, even those who may be their enemies.

b. God wants them to be able to turn the other cheek and do good to those who mistreat them.

c. God wants them to forgive.

d. God wants them to share with and give to others.

12. About other biblical concepts...Children should learn that angels are messengers from God sent to tell people when Jesus was born, to protect God's children, and to do God's work.

a. Fallen angels are the demons that are at work for Satan.

b. Satan will do anything within his power to cause us to sin and he will tempt us to disobey.

B.   9-Year-Olds: For the most part, they like school. They are apt to forget things unless reminded.

      1.   They are critical of things they think they could do better.

Praise

C.   10-Year-Olds: They are fond of friends and like to tell people who they are.

    1.   Simple companionship rather than competition motivates this group.

    2.   Physical stamina is at a higher level.

D.   11-Year-Olds: Peers continue to take up more of their time at this stage.

    1.   They can often seem intense and can fly into a rage at short notice.

    2.   Acceptance is very important to them.

Praise

E.   12-Year-Olds

1.   About God...Children should learn that God is all powerful, all knowing, is everywhere, and is with them at all times.

a. He loves them and wants to have a relationship with them. He wants them to know that each of them is special in His sight. God cares for and loves their families too.

b. God wants them to talk with Him in prayer every day. He always answers prayer with "yes," "no" or "wait." He provides all they need. He can be trusted for all things.

c. God desires their worship. He wants them to trust Him in all their needs and problems, and be thankful for all He has done and is doing in their lives. God wants them to be obedient to their parents and those in authority.

d. God wants them to share His love with others. He wants them to go to His Word to learn about Him, to hear His voice through the Word, and to learn how to live their lives for Him.

2.   About Jesus...Children should learn that He wants to be their Lord and Savior.

a. Through His death on the Cross, Jesus conquered sin and death once and for all. He can and desires to forgive them of their sins. Jesus will grant salvation to all who ask, and He loves them even when they sin.

b. Jesus wants them to be His disciples, follow Him and do His works that He commanded us to do. Jesus is the only way to God and Heaven. He loves them and is their best friend.

c. Jesus wants them to love and obey Him with all of their hearts, souls, minds, and strength.

3.   About the Holy Spirit...Children should learn that when Jesus went to Heaven He sent the Holy Spirit as our comforter and teacher.

a. The Holy Spirit will give us the power and desire to do the Father's will. Through the Holy Spirit we can participate in the things that Jesus did and told us to do.

b. The Holy Spirit will speak to our hearts and show us where there is sin. He will help us worship the Lord and give us things to say to the Lord. It is through the work of the Holy Spirit that we will see healings, miracles, and changed lives.

c. Through the power of the Holy Spirit others will come to know Jesus. They can operate in the gifts of the Spirit. God wants us to live by the fruit of the Spirit.

4. About the Bible...Children should learn that it is God's Word to them and it will reveal the truth to all their questions.

a. The Bible tells them what God wants for them to know and how they are to live their lives for Him.

b. The Bible reveals His perfect love for them. It tells them about how He related to others and showed mankind that He desired to bring us back to Him.

c. It tells them about who they are and why they were created. The Bible was written by the hands of men chosen by God and inspired by the Holy Spirit to write what God told them.

d. The Bible has two major parts called the Old Testament and New Testament. There are sixty-six books in the Bible.

e. The gospels (Matthew, Mark, Luke and John) tell of the life and works of Jesus. They should know the groupings of the other major writings of the Bible.

f. They should read and memorize the Scriptures so they will be strengthened by God's Word to them.

5. About home and parents...Children should learn that God gave them parents to care for them and bring them up in the ways of the Lord.

a. If their parents are non-believers they are to still honor and obey their parents. Our parents love us and we should love them.

b. God cares for their families and each member in their families. Parents have rules to follow and we should obey them.

c. God wants to be the authority in each household. Children should know that they can ask God for help in restoring their family situations, and that God cares very much about their family situations.

6. About church...Children should learn that church is a place to worship and to learn about God.

a. It is a place for them to be equipped and trained as a part of the Christian body. Church should be a place where they feel secure and loved.

7. About others...Children should learn that God loves all people equally, whether or not they believe in Christ.

a. God wants children to learn how to show love and compassion for people.

b. They should know how to lead others to Christ, and to pray for friends and peers. Children should know that they can minister to others.

8. About other biblical concepts...Children should learn about Bible truths, including the nature of sin, the forgiveness of God through Christ, baptism, communion, death and Heaven.

a. They should be taught about Satan, and how he is the tempter and deceiver.

b. They should know that God has power over all things, including the works of Satan. Children should also learn about Christ's Second Coming, and how that affects their lives.

II.   BASIC COMMUNICATION TIPS

The following outline may help you in better understanding how to communicate with your children and students. Each child should be treated as an individual. They may react in different ways to different types of communication.

    A. Respect children.

    B. Talk to children.

        a. Do not interrogate them.

        b. Do not conduct an interview.

        c. Do not preach.

        d. Simply hold a conversation with them.

        e. Make them feel better about themselves.

    C. Listen to children.

        a. Get on their level.

        i. Physically

        ii. In vocabulary - use words they can understand

    b. Listen completely to the whole story.

    c. Listen for attitudes, values, and feelings.

D. Simple reminders:

    a. Treat every child with respect and as an individual.

    b. Be sincere, as with a friend.

    c. Do not be impatient.

    d. Do not jump to obvious answers or conclusions.

    e. Do not be too quick to quote the Bible or give simple answers.

    f. Balance talking and listening.

    g. Evaluate your conversation.

Sometimes we experience difficulty in relating to or communicating with a child. The following is a list of some possible roadblocks to effective communication.

Verbal Roadblocks

A. Ordering or commanding. Examples: "Get down" or "Stop that."

B. Admonishing. Examples: "You should…" or "You ought to…"

C. Judging.

    a. Positive judging. Example: "You are right."

b. Negative judging. Example: "You made a mistake."

D. Using logic. Example: "What you need to know is..."

E. Name calling. Examples: "Lazy" or "Selfish" or "Stupid"

F. Interpreting. Example: "You feel this way because..."

G. Interrogating and probing. Example: Asking "Who, What, Why, When, Where"

H. Advising. Example: "I'll tell you what to do..."

I. Comparing. Example: "When I was your age..."

Non-Verbal Roadblocks

A. Preaching tone of voice

B. Condescending tone

C. Looking away, looking bored

D. Fixed smile

E. No eye contact

Children's Equipping Center
International House of Prayer in Kansas City

The Children's Equipping Center (CEC) has set out to establish a culture that equips children to live fully devoted to God. The CEC's highest priority is to pass on to the next generation the values, programs and practices that are foundational to IHOP-KC and its environment of 24-hour-a-day, night and day prayer and worship.

The Children's Equipping Center develops opportunities for children of all ages to develop and be released into their gifts as musicians, singers, artists, dancers and intercessors. It seeks to enable them to understand the power of the Holy spirit through praying, healing, preaching, teaching, giving to the poor, and reaching the lost through evangelism and missions.

> "We are committed in these days ahead to doing whatever we can to help young people pursue a lifelong passion for Jesus. It is the desire of Lenny and Tracy La Guardia and their staff who serve the Children's Equipping Center that young people experience the power and ministry of the Holy Spirit and walk out their lives knowing that they are truly a 'Friend of the Bridegroom.' Lenny and Tracy have dedicated more than twenty years of their lives to children, leaders and churches all over the world. I encourage you to allow the Children's Equipping Center to bless you as it has the children and families here in Kansas City."

—Mike Bickle, Director
International House of Prayer, Kansas City, Missouri

CEC Directors Lenny & Tracy La Guardia

For two decades, Lenny and Tracy La Guardia have devoted their lives to equipping, empowering, enabling and mobilizing today's young people, parents, and leaders by communicating and putting into place Kingdom of God truths and relevant strategies for ministry to children today.

The La Guardia's passion for mobilizing this generation of children and young people to walk in the fullness of Christ and in the power of the Holy Spirit has taken them all over the world as speakers and consultants to thousands. In their senior staff capacity at the International House of Prayer Missions Base in Kansas City, under the leadership of Mike Bickle, they direct and oversee all local, national and international ministries relating to children and teens. They have been married 25 years and have five children, Lenny, Leatha, Andrea, Adrienne and Shontavion. To request that Lenny or Tracy speak or consult at your church or event, or to host a Children's Prophetic Leadership Summit, please e-mail your invitation to equipchildren@ihop.org.

Children's Equipping Center Annual Events

National Children's Equipping Conference
Held every September, this conference seeks to further CEC's goal of equipping a generation to receive and experience God's love and to love God in return. This conference also fulfills CEC's call to gather parents and others who lead children and desire to equip an end-time army of forerunners.

Like never before, we have the opportunity and responsibility to train, equip and prepare young forerunners to passionately pursue the Lord, and to release them into their God-given destinies. This yearly event covers topics that impact and change the hearts and lives of parents, children's and junior high school pastors, leaders, and teachers. Teaching tracks and breakout sessions are designed to equip attendees with strategies and truths that will help them do their part in releasing this generation in prayer, praise, power and the prophetic. There are additional breakout sessions on leadership and resource development, ministry to toddlers and preschoolers, releasing children in worship and praise, the ministry of the Holy Spirit, and signs and wonders.

Children of all ages are welcome, though no childcare is available. There is a children's equipping track for ages 6-12. Ages 1-5 are welcome to attend the main sessions with their parents. There is a pre-conference lunch held on the Friday before the conference. For costs, conference details, registration and a sample schedule, please visit *www.IHOP.org.*

Releasing Children in Power & Praise
This two-day seminar held three times a year is an opportunity for parents and leaders to be equipped side-by-side with their children and youth for worship and intercession. Explore the gifts and power of the Holy Spirit that are released when His people lift up God's praises. The weekend includes teaching and practical experience for children and adults in the Harp & Bowl model of prayer. There is no childcare provided. For costs, seminar details, registration and a sample schedule, please visit *www.IHOP.org.*

Leadership Summit: Changing Paradigms of Ministry to Children
The goal of this summit is for leaders, pastors and parents to get refreshed in the prayer room and equipped and retooled for their ministries. Summits have a relaxed atmosphere with more personal ministry and teaching and are held quarterly. There is no childcare provided. There are group discounts. For costs, details and registration, please visit *www.IHOP.org.*

Signs & Wonders Camps

These camps are offered at locations in Kansas City, Mississippi and Colorado. Children 8 to 12 years old receive training, teaching and practical experience walking with the Holy Spirit and ministering in power. This is coupled with the fun and recreation of summer camp. There are group discounts available and costs include food, lodging, teaching workbook and more. For costs, details, dates and downloadable registration forms, please visit *www.IHOP.org.*

Summer Teen Intensive

Held each summer, the intensive is a three-week program aimed at equipping teens in prophetic worship, intercession, intimacy with Jesus, and the great commission. Group discounts are available. Tuition includes all meals, lodging, materials and more. For costs, details, dates and a downloadable application, please visit *www.ihop.org.*